Peking Opera costume

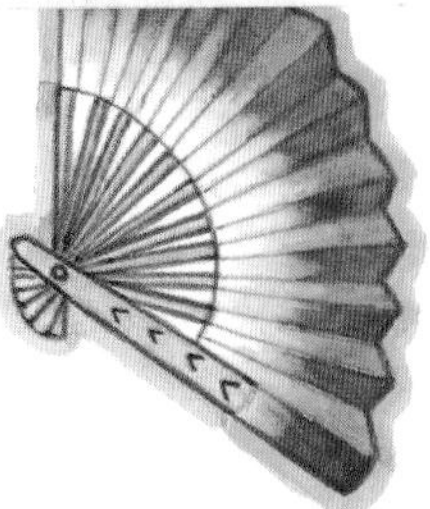

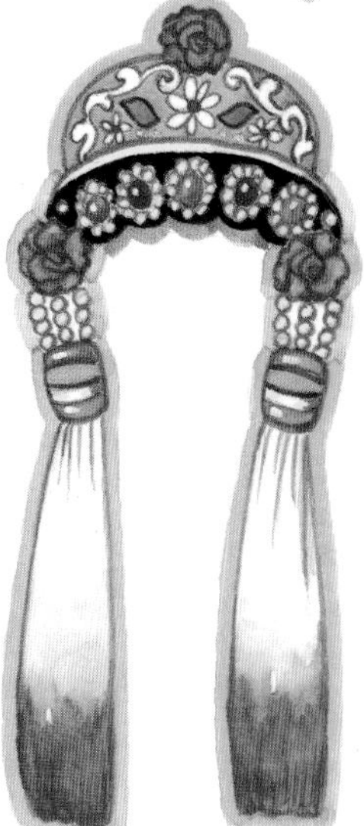

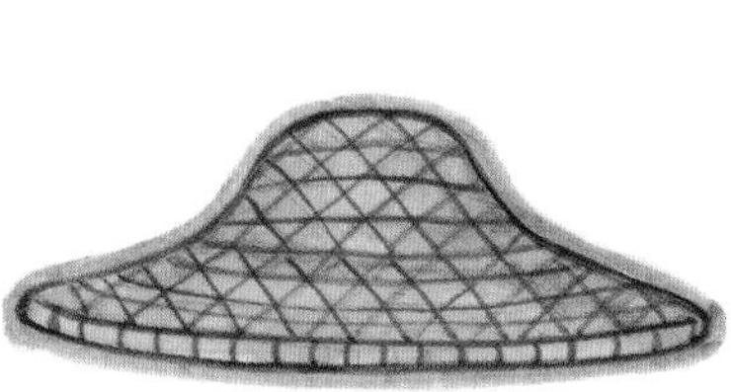

Hair ornament

New Year's costume

Court costume

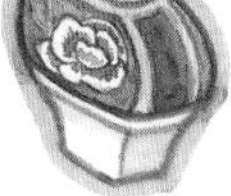

Mongolian costume ↓

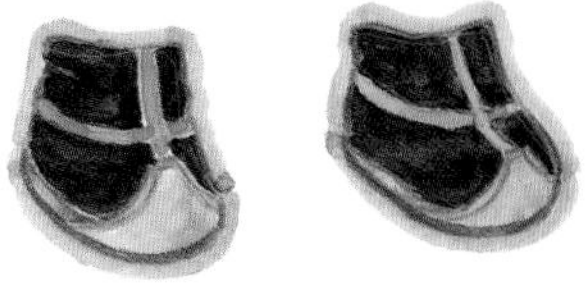

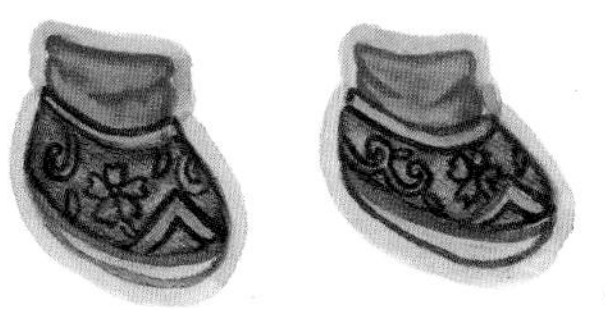

↑ Tibetan costume

Embroidered costume

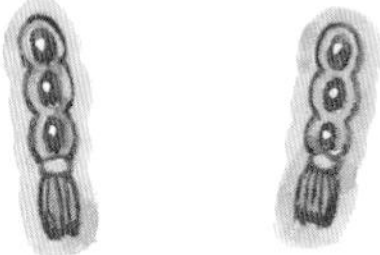

Panda doll

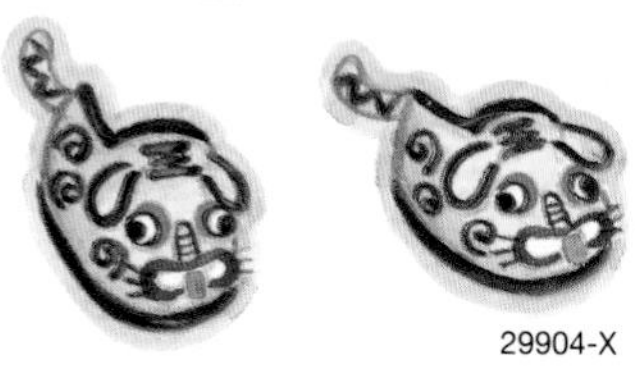

29904-X